INVERTEBRATES

Please visit our web site at: **www.garethstevens.com**
For a free color catalog describing Gareth Stevens Publishing's list of high-quality books and multimedia programs, call **1-800-542-2595 (USA)** or **1-800-387-3178 (Canada)**. Gareth Stevens Publishing's fax: **(414) 332-3567**.

Library of Congress Cataloging-in-Publication Data

Spineless.
    Invertebrates.
        p. cm. — (Discovery Channel school science: the plant and animal kingdoms)
    Contents: Invertebrates—Blob blab—Spineless wonders—Squid hunt—Old-timers—Come out of your shell—Aquanauts to the rescue!—Masters of disguise—Pesty critters—Go, bug, go!—Spare parts—Dirt digger—Treasure-hunt horrors—Spineless lives—Invertebrates unite.
    ISBN 0-8368-3216-7 (lib. bdg.)
    1. Invertebrates—Juvenile literature. [1. Invertebrates.] I. Title. II. Series.
QL362.4.S65   2002
592—dc21   2002023873

This edition first published in 2002 by
Gareth Stevens Publishing
A World Almanac Education Group Company
330 West Olive Street, Suite 100
Milwaukee, WI 53212 USA

Writers: Jackie Ball, Margaret Carruthers, Kathleen Feeley, Sara Heiberger, Katie King, Kim King, Lisa Krause, Monique Peterson, Darcy Sharon, Denise Vega.

Editor: Katie King.

Photographs: Cover, snail, © James H Robinson/Photo Researchers, Inc.; p. 2, starfish, Corel; p. 3, aquanauts, © Giacomo Bernardi; p. 4, sponge, starfish, sea anemone (all), Corel, roundworm, © Cabisco/Visuals Unlimited; p. 5, flatworm, © William C. Jorgenson/Visuals Unlimited, scorpion, Corel, earthworm, © Jeff Daly/Visuals Unlimited, snail, CORBIS; p. 6, jellyfish, Discovery Communications, Inc./NOAA; p. 8, lobster, Corel; p. 9, sea anemone, caterpillar (both), Corel; pp. 10–11, squid engraving, Culver Pictures; p. 10, Clyde Roper, © I. H. Roper; p. 11, giant squid, © I. H. Roper; p. 12, Grand Canyon, Corel, trilobite, PhotoDisc; p. 13, geologist, PhotoDisc; p. 14, Steinbeck portrait, Archive Photos, pearl, Corel; p. 15, cowrie shell, spiral shell, Huichol Indian (all), Corel; p. 16, diagram of *Aquarius*, NOAA; coral, Corel; p. 17, aquanauts, © Giacomo Bernardi, divers outside *Aquarius*, © Giacomo Bernardi; p. 18, crab, © Hal Beral/Visuals

This U.S. edition © 2002 by Gareth Stevens, Inc. First published in 2001 as *Spineless: The Invertebrate Files* by Discovery Enterprises, LLC, Bethesda, Maryland. © 2001 by Discovery Communications, Inc.

Further resources for students and educators available at www.discoveryschool.com

Designed by Bill SMITH STUDIO
Project Editors: Justine Ciovacco, Katie King, Anna Prokos
Designers: Sonia Gauba, Dmitri Kushnirsky, Jay Jaffe, Eric Hoffsten
Photo Editors: Sean Livingstone, Christie K. Silver
Intern: Chris Pascarella
Art Buyer: Lillie Caporlingua
Gareth Stevens Editor: Alan Wachtel
Gareth Stevens Art Director: Tammy Gruenewald

Printed in the United States of America

1 2 3 4 5 6 7 8 9 06 05 04 03 02

Unlimited, cuttlefish, © Wolcott Henry/Discovery Communications, Inc.; p. 19, dog whelk, © Gustav Verdeber/Visuals Unlimited, caterpillar, walkingstick (both), Corel, shrimp, © P. M. David/Photo Researchers, Inc.; p. 20, sea urchin, PhotoDisc, diver, Corel; p. 21, fruitfly, PhotoDisc, hikers, Corel; p. 22, Robert Full, © Noah Berger, centipede on treadmill, Rhex robot, Image 2000 Peter Menzel/*Robo sapiens*; p. 24, octopus, PhotoDisc; p. 25, starfish, © Kjell B. Sandved/Visuals Unlimited, flatworm, © Dave B. Fleetham/Visuals Unlimited; pp. 26–27, worm, © R. F. Ashley/Visuals Unlimited; p. 29, daddy longlegs, © Bill Beatty/Visuals Unlimited, tick, © Robert Calentine/Visuals Unlimited, brown recluse spider, © Rob & Ann Simpson/Visuals Unlimited; p. 30, sponge, Corel, brittlestars, K. B. Sandved/Visuals Unlimited; p. 31, lobster, squid, limpet (all), Corel.

Acknowledgments: p. 14, excerpt from THE PEARL by John Steinbeck © 1945, Viking Press; p. 22, centipede and Rhex photographs from the book ROBO SAPIENS: EVOLUTION OF A NEW SPECIES by Peter Menzel and Faith D'Aluisio. A Material World Book. The MIT Press, Fall 2000.

CONTENTS

INVERTEBRATES

Look around you. Worms bury themselves in the soil. Horseshoe crabs and sand dollars wash up on the beach. On a walk through the woods you may notice insects busily working. No matter where you go, chances are you'll meet up with an invertebrate of one kind or another.

Invertebrates are creatures that do not have backbones. You and I cannot survive without a backbone. But invertebrates have been around a long time because they are well-adapted to their environments. That's what makes them fascinating. Invertebrates do what all animals do—grow, reproduce, and survive—and they do it all without a spine. Learn why it's important to get to know these creatures better. Join Discovery Channel's INVERTEBRATES on a tour of this amazing corner of the animal kingdom.

Invertebrates 4
At-a-Glance Invertebrates may be spineless, but they have unique structures to help them survive.

Blob Blab 6
Q & A A soft jellyfish is tough enough to survive in its environment.

Spineless Wonders 8
Almanac Invertebrates are diverse. Find out how this group of animals compares with others in the animal kingdom.

Squid Hunt 10
Eyewitness Account Scientist Clyde Roper has spent many years searching for the giant squid.

Old-Timers 12
Timeline Visit the Grand Canyon to travel back in time and learn how an invertebrate becomes a fossil.

Come Out of Your Shell 14
Scrapbook Invertebrates may not stick around for long, but their shells do! Find out how people have used shells for thousands of years.

Aquanauts to the Rescue! 16
Heroes Spend a few days underwater in the *Aquarius* sea lab with scientists who are working to save a coral reef.

Aquanauts live in the deep blue sea. See page 17.

Masters of Disguise 18

Picture This They can't run for cover, but these invertebrates have ways to protect themselves.

Pesty Critters 20

Map See how insects, shellfish, and worms can harm whole ecosystems.

Go, Bug, Go! 22

Scientist's Notebook Robert J. Full studies cockroaches, crabs, and other invertebrates to help design the next generation of robots.

Spare Parts 24

Amazing but True Lost an arm or a leg? That's not a problem for the invertebrates that can grow new ones.

Dirt Digger 26

Virtual Voyage You're an earthworm about to make a journey deep into the ground.

Treasure-Hunt Horrors. 28

Solve-It-Yourself Mystery Poking around old Widow Fiddleboch's woodshed for treasures, Perry and his friends get more than they bargained for. What's hiding in dark places?

Spineless Lives 30

Fun & Fantastic Check out some of the interesting ways that invertebrates get to know each other and defend themselves.

Final Project

Invertebrates Unite 32

Your World, Your Turn Students focus on one ecosystem and study the invertebrates that live there.

Invertebrates

Sponges

Orange sponge

Roundworms

Hookworm

When someone says "animal," you might picture a cat, dog, horse, bird, or tiger. But what about a worm, starfish, or spider? Scientists call these animals invertebrates because they have no vertebrae, or backbones. They and all other invertebrates are spineless.

Scientists have identified close to one million invertebrate species, which they place into eight phyla, or categories. The phyla are named on these pages, and one animal species in each group is pictured. The categories of invertebrates contain a wide range of animals, from sponges and segmented worms to spiders and jellyfish, but all these animals have something in common: They have adapted traits that help them survive successfully without backbones in their environments.

Take the flatworm. This one-and-a-half-inch-long invertebrate lives in damp soil, streams, and oceans. The flatworm can do what most vertebrates can't. It can regrow a lost or damaged body part. If a flatworm loses part of its body while

Starfish

Echinoderms
(ee-KINE-uh-derms)

Cnidarians (nye-DAIR-ee-uhns)

Pink sea anemone

struggling with a predator, it grows a new part. You won't ever see a tiger or a lion grow a new leg.

A marine invertebrate with a soft, jellylike body, the sea anemone (uh-NEM-uh-nee) looks like a flower and spends most of its life in one place. Sounds harmless, but the anemone is a predator. Clinging to a rock, it waits for its prey—usually a fish—stings it with poisonous tentacles, and pushes the prey into its mouth.

Insects are invertebrates, too. Ants, and many other insects, have developed body structures that have helped them survive. A hard outer covering protects an ant's internal organs. Ants are strong, too; an ant can carry 50 times its own body weight. How does it do it? Even though ants don't weigh much, they have proportionally more muscle mass than most animals, so they can lift heavy things. Their tiny size allows ants to live in all kinds of places—trees, underground tunnels, inside plants, and even inside the walls of houses.

It's no wonder that invertebrates make up a large part of the animal kingdom and live in practically every ecosystem.

Mollusks

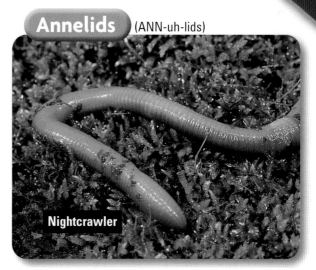
Snail

Annelids (ANN-uh-lids)

Nightcrawler

Flatworms

Marine flatworm

Arthropods

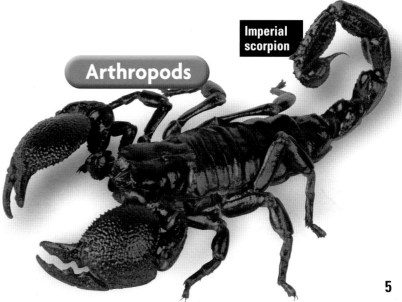
Imperial scorpion

5

BLOB BLAB

An interview with an outspoken representative of invertebrates

Q: Hey! You out there! Umbrella-parachute-looking thing with strings hanging down! Got a minute?
A: After that charming description, I'm not so sure. But what's up?

Q: We're from "Invertebrates at Work and Play," a new lifestyle cable show, and we need an invertebrate to interview. Do you know any?
A: Of course! I myself am an invertebrate—a jellyfish, to be exact.

Q: Jellyfish . . . does that mean you're some kind of fish?
A: No. I should really be called a jelly. I'm part of the phylum Cnidaria (nye-DAIR-ee-uh), which includes corals, sea anemones, and hydras. Sometimes it's called the coelenterate (sih-LEN-ter-ate) phylum.

Q: Oh, of course! Great! So come on in to shore, and we'll get you into makeup—that will be challenging—and then on camera.
A: Uh, no can do.

Q: Why not?
A: Because in minutes you'd be interviewing a damp spot on the sand. Jellyfish are 98 percent water. My see-through, jellylike body is supported by water. When I'm not in the ocean, I can't maintain my shape, can't move. Kaput.

Q: But some invertebrates live on land, don't they?
A: Lots of them do. But they have different equipment. As a group, invertebrates are kind of a mish-mash. We make up about

96 percent of all animal species, but we all have different looks and lifestyles, not to mention different body parts, organization, and structures. About the only thing that groups us together is what we don't have—a backbone.

Q: **Hmm. Must be tough to get around without a skeleton.**
A: Wait, wait. I didn't say we don't have a skeleton. I said a backbone. There's a difference. We all have skeletons.

Q: **But YOU don't have a skeleton, do you? You look so soft.**
A: Don't be fooled by the beautiful, dreamy, floating image. I'm tougher than I look. This whole center part of me, practically my whole body, not counting the tentacles, is my skeleton. I have a muscular ring around the outside of my body. It does a good job of keeping me together and helping me move. When I squeeze my muscle, I suck in seawater through the opening at my bottom, which is my mouth. When I relax my muscle, the water shoots out, propelling me forward.

Q: **Sounds efficient.**
A: It's OK. But, sometimes, I wish I had an exoskeleton, a hard outer skeleton, to protect me. Arthropods and mollusks, like beetles and snails, have them. They're like hard shells.

Q: **Why do you want a shell?**
A: One word: protection. Those hard coverings are like armor, keeping internal organs and all the other soft stuff tucked safely inside. If I had one, I could probably go ashore without collapsing or drying up. I could

hide in my shell so a predator wouldn't munch on my insides, which are all open and exposed. But it's not as if I don't have special defenses of my own. My poisonous, stinging tentacles keep away unwanted attention, such as predators. I also use them to sting and paralyze my prey and draw it into my inner digestive cavity, where it gets absorbed.

Q: **Any other advantages to exoskeletons?**
A: Well, any rigid skeleton provides support and helps muscles move efficiently. There's more resistance for muscles to pull against. Spiders, crabs, and insects all can move in more ways than I can. Exoskeletons helped animals move onto land. It was a real advance. But I have to be content with the squeeze, relax, squeeze, relax thing. At least I don't have to molt.

Q: **What's molting?**
A: It's another name for shedding your shell or outside covering. See, exoskeletons don't grow, so as animals get bigger, they need to make bigger shells and get rid of the old ones that don't fit anymore.

Q: **Sounds like it would get tiresome after a while.**
A: Well, you humans won't ever have to worry about it. Mammals, birds, reptiles, fish, and amphibians

are vertebrates. The backbones and limbs and stuff that make up your skeleton are inside, and it grows right along with you. When you break a bone, it repairs itself.

Q: **So it's best to be a vertebrate to survive in this world?**
A: I don't know about that. Your outside—your skin—doesn't offer that much protection. You're exposed to weather and danger all the time. There's no hard coating protecting your internal organs any more than there is protecting mine. And some invertebrates have a neat trick up their sleeves, something very few vertebrates can do.

Q: **What's that?**
A: They have the ability to grow new parts. Flatworms can grow new heads. Starfish can grow new arms.

Q: **Cool.**
A: Yes, but, speaking of cool, I've got to be going. Cool waves to float on. Prey to sting, poison, and eat! Same old, same old. But it's a living.

Q: **OK, thanks for your time. Any last thoughts on being spineless?**
A: Invertebrates have been around more than 600 million years. You don't survive that long unless you're doing something right. So don't sell spinelessness short.

Activity

SUPPORT SYSTEM A skeleton is the framework for a body. A skeleton gives support. It also protects internal organs. Exoskeletons are outside the body, and endoskeletons are inside. List 10 animals that have an exoskeleton. What other traits do all these animals share? List 10 animals that have an endoskeleton. What traits do all these animals share? Are invertebrates on either list?

SPINELESS Wonders

You can find invertebrates in oceans, ponds, rivers, or even crawling in your backyard. These creatures are a diverse group—and a huge part of the animal kingdom!

TRY THIS ON FOR SIZE

Scientists think there are more than 1 million species of animals on Earth. Of that number, invertebrates are clearly in the majority.

INVERTEBRATES
Total Species: about 980,000

In the invertebrate world, insects may be small, but they dominate.

Coelenterates (jellyfish, corals, comb jellies) **0.9%**

Segmented Worms (earthworms, etc.) **1%**

Hookworms (rotifers, etc.) **1%**

Flatworms (tapeworms, etc.) **2%**

Mollusks 5%

Arthropods (mites, spiders, crustaceans, etc.) **12%**

Echinoderms (starfish, sea urchins, etc.) **0.6%**

Porifera (sponges) **0.5%**

Insects 74%

ALL ANIMALS
Total Species: over 1,000,000

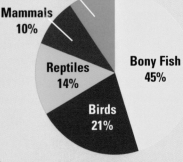

Lobster

VERTEBRATES
Total Species: about 42,000

Amphibians 10%

Mammals 10%

Reptiles 14%

Bony Fish 45%

Birds 21%

NO SHELTER

Invertebrates, such as decorator crabs, camouflage themselves with discarded shells and alga bits for protection from predators. Other invertebrates rely on different defenses.

sea slug This critter has a terrible taste.

sea anemone Its numerous stinging tentacles paralyze the enemy.

sea urchin Sharp, poisonous spines protect this creature.

chiton When in danger, this mollusk rolls itself into a ball.

razor clam It is good at burying itself in the sand.

sea spider It has 10 to 12 pairs of long walking legs with sharp claws.

sea cucumber It ejects sticky white threads from its back end to confuse its prey.

Black swallowtail caterpillar

Pink sea anemone

HOW DO THEY MEASURE UP?

Even the tiniest invertebrates are busy critters.

The Producers
About 2,500 silkworms produce one pound of silk.

Muscles Galore
On average, a caterpillar has 4,000 muscles; a human has 792.

Here a Worm, There a Worm
Worms come in all sizes.

Full-grown beef tapeworm (Flatworm)	80 feet (24 m)—as long as two city buses
Giant earthworm (Segmented worm)	12 feet (3.5 m)—can stretch to 21 feet (6.5 m), or as long as your classroom
Tube worms	4 feet (1.2 m)—about as long as you are tall
Most flatworms	Less than 2 inches (5 cm)— as long as your pinkie
Some roundworms	0.008 inches (0.2 mm)— a period at the end of a sentence
Parasitic roundworm (*Ascaris lumbricoides*)	Can grow 19 inches (48 cm) in length

Going the Distance

Invertebrates know how to make up for lost time.

▶ A **dragonfly** may travel at the speed of 35 miles (56 km) an hour.

▶ A **deer botfly** travels up to 36 miles (58 km) an hour.

▶ **Snails** glide about 10 feet (3 m) an hour on trails of slimy mucus.

▶ Some **squid** can jump out of water and land 100 feet (30 m) away.

▶ A **flea** can jump 300 times its own length.

▶ A male **gypsy moth** can pick up the scent of a female gypsy moth 7 miles (11 km) away.

SQUID HUNT

A biologist searches for a legendary creature no one has ever seen alive.

Clyde Roper, a marine biologist at the National Museum of Natural History in Washington, D.C., travels in *Deep Rover*, a futuristic submersible with a bubblelike front and two robotic arms. The vessel "flies" like an underwater helicopter and takes oceanographers 3,200 feet (975 m) underwater. What is Roper looking for? A giant squid—an invertebrate that can grow up to 60 feet (18 m) long. Roper answers questions about his experiences below.

Q: *How did you get interested in the giant squid?*
A: Late in my graduate studies, I had the opportunity to examine a sperm whale stranded on a beach. We did an autopsy on it, so I got a chance to crawl around inside the whale's three stomachs, which were squishy and still warm. Inside one of its stomachs was a giant squid.

What is it like searching for a giant squid aboard Deep Rover?
It's like scuba diving—but a hundred times more exciting. I get to go into places very few people have entered. In many cases, no one has ever been in these places before. In Kaikoura Canyon, New Zealand, we went down more than 2,300 feet (700 m).

Though we didn't see a squid, we saw things no one had ever seen alive before. Down that deep, it's gorgeous. There are sponges that are orange, red, and

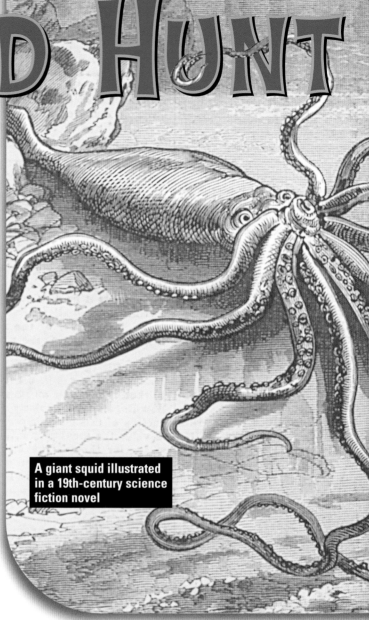

A giant squid illustrated in a 19th-century science fiction novel

white, huge, frilled mussels, deep-sea crabs, and snails. On one dive we saw a pair of prickly sharks. No one had ever seen a pair of them together alive. It's exciting to be down in the inky blackness. We turn off all the lights and glide silently through the water. The creatures in the deep sea have so much bioluminescence, which is the ability to emit their own light, that we don't need lights to see a lot.

Did you ever feel that you were near a squid?
We were absolutely near a giant squid. It's a huge ocean, and our few rays of light penetrated just 15 to 30 feet (4.5 to 9 m). That's it. You really don't know what's right beside you. But after 20 years of studying invertebrates, I pretty much know their

Dr. Clyde Roper

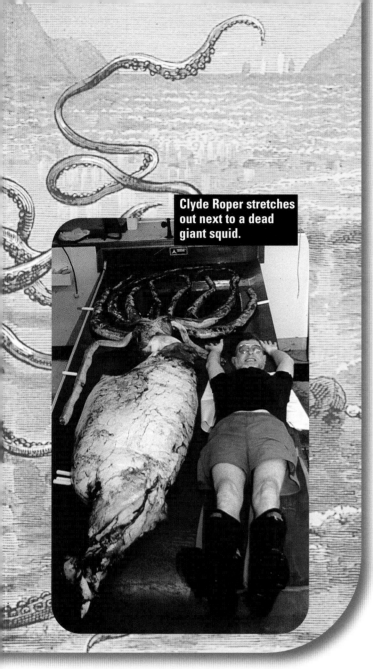

Clyde Roper stretches out next to a dead giant squid.

its exact habitat, its locomotion, and whether it hangs and rests in a horizontal position.

Why do giant squid have such large eyes?
The sea is perpetually dark, and a larger eye will capture more light. These giant eyes might help them detect bioluminescence in the water created by their prey moving about. This is something we have yet to learn about.

What does a giant squid feel like?
Squid feel pretty squishy, although they can be muscular. A giant squid feels semisoft and almost spongy, but smooth, not slimy. Some species are very soft, because they are deep-sea animals, and hard bodies couldn't stand the pressure of the deep sea.

What does a giant squid taste like?
I'm a great believer in using all of our senses to learn. I did taste a piece of a giant squid. It was very bitter and tough. I certainly wouldn't want to have to eat it every day! But, if you ever see it on a menu, you should give it a try.

Do you think you'll look for giant squid again?
Absolutely. Yes. It's impossible to answer every question and solve every problem the first time we try. It took many tries before anyone made it to the top of Mount Everest, so it isn't surprising that we haven't seen a giant squid yet. We think we know so much about life on Earth, but the giant squid is the largest invertebrate ever to have lived on Earth, and no one has ever seen one alive! But what's even more amazing is that there are many thousands of species in the ocean still to be discovered—most just don't happen to be 40 feet (12 m) long. It's crazy, but scientists have been working with submersibles for 50 years. In all of that time, we have still observed less than 50 square miles (130 sq km) of the ocean floor. That's an area smaller than Washington, D.C.

Do you think anyone will ever see a giant squid alive?
Someday someone is going to see one. I hope it's me.

habitat. If I'm in the zone where predators are feeding and in an area where specimens have been netted, I'm feeling pretty confident that I'm in the right place.

What can you learn from a dead squid?
Everything we know about the giant squid so far has come from specimens that have washed up on the beach or have been pulled up in fishermen's nets. We basically perform an autopsy on them. We can determine their sex, their stage of maturity, and whether they've already reproduced. We can also look at their stomach contents to see what they eat.

What could you learn from seeing a live squid?
In just 15 to 20 seconds, I could tell you an awful lot, including the depth that the animal occupies,

Activity

FEELING SQUID-ISH? Imagine you are a scientist in search of a giant squid. What kind of equipment would you need to search for it? Where in the world would you look? What does it feed on, and what are its predators? What would you do if you found a giant squid? Map out your plan for a two-month mission to find the giant squid.

Old-Timers

Ancient trilobite fossils report from the Grand Canyon on life and times long, long ago . . .

Fossils in rock layers are the remains of organisms that lived during earlier time periods in Earth's history. Index fossils help geologists date rock layers. Fossils of trilobites, which were arthropods (like insects and lobsters) that lived in the oceans from 570 to 245 million years ago, make good index fossils. Here's how a trilobite becomes a fossil.

550 MILLION YEARS AGO

LIVING IT UP!

Olenellus (OH-len-ELL-us) lives in the sea in what is now the desert in Arizona. One of the earliest trilobites on Earth, it scurries over the sand and mud near the seashore, feeding on smaller invertebrates. As it grows, it sheds its hard exoskeleton, the structure that surrounds its body. Over time, many trilobites live, shed, and die.

505 MILLION YEARS AGO

DYING OUT

Olenellus becomes extinct. It may evolve into a new genus, or the environment changes and *Olenellus* can't adapt. Whatever the reason, no *Olenellus* leaves behind an exoskeleton in rock layers that form after this period.

Trilobite fossils

A geologist digs up fossils.

What Makes a Good Index Fossil?

Here are the qualities a fossil needs to make the grade.

1. **Widespread:** The original plant or animal must have lived in a large region so that geologists can use it to show a relationship between rocks from different parts of the world.

2. **Short period of time:** If a species survived through more than one geologic era, it won't help pinpoint a rock layer's age.

3. **Abundant and easy to find:** Millions of trilobites left behind a huge number of exoskeletons.

4. **Easy to identify:** Every trilobite species indicates a geologic time period.

5. **Well preserved:** Trilobites became fossils because they had hard shells that did not decay or disintegrate.

505–10 MILLION YEARS AGO

BURIED

Olenellus remains become fossils. More sand and mud layers build up, burying the trilobite exoskeletons deeper and deeper. Other sediments are deposited on top, and the sand and mud particles squeeze together to form a natural cement. To become a fossil, an animal must be completely buried by a very fine sediment. Eventually, minerals replace the calcium in the bone or shell. The sediment hardens into sandstone or shale, with the trilobite fossils locked in.

10 MILLION YEARS AGO–PRESENT

EXPOSED

The sea is long gone. The region is now just a low, flat area with a river running through it that cuts through the rocks. Over time the river makes a canyon, which gets deeper and wider every day. The trilobite skeletons that have been buried for more than 500 million years are exposed on the deep canyon walls. As early as the 1850s, geologists could see which fossils correspond to certain time periods in Earth's history. They come to the Grand Canyon and find *Olenellus* fossils, which tell them that the rock formed about 550 million years ago.

Activity

FOSSIL FINESSE Trilobites are useful index fossils. Research the anatomy, lifestyle, environment, and evolution of these creatures. Discuss why their remains are useful to geologists. What time period(s) can trilobites be used to date? What conclusions can you draw from learning about different trilobites?

13

COME OUT OF YOUR SHELL

Many invertebrate creatures have strong outer shells. Long after these animals die, their hard shells stay around. People have found different uses for shells over the years.

Filter Feeders

A bivalve is an animal such as a clam or oyster that lives in a shell made of two halves. Many bivalves live in waters with strong currents, so they attach themselves to rocks. There they stay, filtering water and particles through their bodies to get their food.

A Pearl is Born! Most bivalves protect themselves by filtering out foreign objects such as tiny shell or coral pieces. But pearl oysters don't filter as quickly as other bivalves. As a result, they create pearls.

If an object gets trapped inside the animal's delicate flesh, the animal adapts by covering the object with nacre, the material from the inner part of its shell (below). The nacre builds up in thick layers, and, after a few years, this growth makes a pearl.

SPIRAL WORLDS

A mollusk begins its life as a larva and builds its shell by depositing calcium from the mantle, or fleshy fold, on its body. As the animal grows, its shell moves outward in a spiral shape. After a while many spiral mollusks stop growing. If they begin to grow again, their shells display a variety of marks. These marks help scientists identify different mollusk species.

Pearls come in all sizes. In *The Pearl*, a short story by John Steinbeck, Kino is a diver who finds a large pearl. He hopes it will bring him a better life.

John Steinbeck

Kino lifted the flesh [of the oyster], and there it lay, the great pearl, perfect as the moon. It captured the light and refined it and gave it back in silver incandescence. It was as large as a seagull's egg. It was the greatest pearl in the world.

THE SHELL TRADE

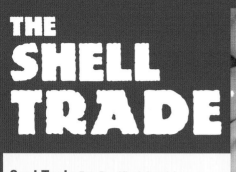

Cool Tools For Pacific Islanders, shells were once crucial to living. People used the shells of the giant clam to make tools for clearing land or preparing food. They made chisels for fine woodworking from the Bullmouth Helmut shell.

Money Talks In Asia, Europe, and Africa, people once used shells as money, too. They bought goods and services and paid for brides and funeral rites with the shells of cowries (COW-rees), which are a kind of marine gastropod. These shells have brilliant colors because cowries eat algae from reefs. Most live on rocks close to shore, where ocean waves pound over them. This makes cowries very shiny and smooth and all about the same size. Unlike a bivalve, which has two parts, a cowrie has one tiny slit where the animal hides, so its shell is strong and less likely to break. These qualities made cowries easy to carry and impossible to counterfeit.

Sound Off! As the triton grows larger, growth marks show on its shell. As it gets older, the triton stops making spirals and lays down more calcium to make a thicker shell. Without as many spirals, more air flows in the shell, creating a perfect wind instrument. Fiji Islanders blew the triton's trumpet before battle and during funeral rites. They also used it for communication.

Fast Movers

Gastropods know how to get around. True to their name, which means "stomach-foot," gastropods scrape over rocks and hard surfaces on their stomachs. This movement creates the bold patterns on their shells.

A DRIFTER

A nautilus grows differently from most mollusks. As the animal grows, its shell grows outward, forming a spiral shape. But each section in the spiral gets sealed off. This creates chambers filled with gas that help the nautilus float. The animal lets water in or out to control its buoyancy.

Nautilus

Once a year, the Huichol Indians in central Mexico blow the murex shell during a feast. The sound signals the gods that the corn is ready to harvest.

AQUANAUTS to the Rescue!

Key Largo, Florida, 2000

In an underwater lab, scientists work to save a coral reef.

A coral reef is a delicate ecosystem, vulnerable to outside factors that can alter and harm the relationships among its marine species. Many of the world's coral reefs suffer from pollution, overfishing, and some effects of global warming. Sometimes people remove corals from the water because they don't know that corals are tiny animals.

Aquarius, an underwater lab, lies 50 feet (15 m) below the ocean's surface. This 81 ton (73.5 m. ton) research facility is the only one of its kind. Living inside are six aquanauts, scientists who are working to protect Florida's Conch Reef from extinction. The scientists on *Aquarius* make it their business to learn everything they can about coral reefs. They know that whole ecosystems depend on coral reefs, which take hundreds, or thousands, of years to form. Millions of corals, which are tiny, tentacled invertebrates, make up one reef. Living in colonies, the corals build hard, chalky, cuplike homes made of calcium carbonate to hide in during the day. At night they wave their stinging tentacles to capture food. When a coral dies, it leaves its stony home behind, where another coral builds a new home. Algae that live inside the coral give it color and provide food for it. The coral reef provides a habitat and food for fish, algae, and sea plants. These species depend on the coral for survival, just as the coral depends on them.

Red fan coral

An artist's view of *Aquarius* on the seafloor

Scientists swim outside *Aquarius*.

Aquanauts relax inside *Aquarius*.

Gathering Crucial Data

Aquarius aquanauts can spend days underwater, so they can gather lots of data. They have discovered that ultraviolet light damages coral reefs. They have also made geological surveys, studied coral feeding patterns, and evaluated pollution levels. They study the reefs over time to observe natural changes, as well as the long-term effects of pollution.

Sometimes the aquanauts show off their lab to students during live chats on the Internet. Aquanaut Mark Patterson has told thousands of students his favorite thing about living underwater is that he can study the reef for hours without going up to the surface for oxygen. "Sometimes," he says, "I feel like I'm a marine mammal!"

Submerged

On a recent *Aquarius* expedition, the aquanauts studied *Halimeda*, a green seaweed common in coral reef environments. White beach sand in the Florida Keys is mostly made of calcium carbonate produced when the seaweed dies and breaks apart. Seaweed is an important part of the coral reef community. Many fish feed on it.

But too much seaweed smothers the coral. *Halimeda* is fast-growing, and scientists are trying to figure out how it affects the larger food web in the Keys. In the predawn darkness, the aquanauts leave their lab to watch nocturnal sea urchins feed on the seaweed. The scientists want to see how fast the seaweed grows, how it reproduces, and what other creatures feed on it.

At the end of their stay aboard *Aquarius*, the scientists pack up all their data to analyze at their labs. They will use this data to educate the public and other scientists about ways to protect coral reefs.

A few days later, a new team of aquanauts descends to *Aquarius* in a continuing quest to save the world's coral reefs.

ENDANGERED CORAL REEFS

Just like the disappearing rain forests, coral reefs in the world's tropical waters are threatened by human and environmental factors. Nearly 25 percent of the world's reefs have disappeared. The rest face great danger.

Corals are animals that thrive in clean, warm water that is shallow enough to let in sunlight. Mining, farming, and logging on coastal land can cause soil to erode and rush downstream into nearby waters. Soil runoff blocks the sunlight, smothering the coral and the tiny algae that are crucial to coral health.

Pollution hurts coral, too. Fertilizers, sewage, and toxic industrial chemicals that find their way into the ocean harm the coral and the hundreds of species of fish and plants that rely on the coral reef ecosystem. Overfishing also upsets a reef's natural balance. When the large fish that eat smaller fish disappear, the coral may be gobbled up by too many of its small, fishy predators.

People sometimes take coral pieces to sell or keep as souvenirs. Occasionally, boaters drop their anchors on coral, which crushes the animals and ruins the reef forever. You can help preserve coral reefs. Tell your friends and family not to touch coral, buy coral jewelry, or use coral in a fish aquarium.

Activity

SAVE THE SPINELESS! Do you know of any other invertebrates that are endangered? Visit a natural history museum or find information about invertebrates in the library or on the Internet to identify one species that is in trouble. Write a profile of this species, including information about its habitat, prey, predators, reproduction, and the factors that threaten its survival. Then write a proposal describing ways to save the species from extinction.

MASTERS OF DISGUISE

Like all living things, invertebrates have adapted special features to help them survive. Many have protective shells, while others have innovative ways of catching prey and avoiding predators.

Sitting Pretty: Crabs

Camouflage helps many crabs blend into their surroundings. The ghost crab is the same color as white beach sand. Just like a ghost, it can disappear. The decorator crab (right) gathers bits of algae, sponges, and animal pieces to attach to its shell. Once it's "decorated," the crab is hard for predators to spot.

Decorator crab

Color Me Beautiful: Cuttlefish

Cuttlefish

Cuttlefish protect themselves by confusing and distracting their prey. Thanks to pigment cells in their skin, cuttlefish can quickly change color, shade, and brightness. When a cuttlefish senses danger, the animal contracts its muscles, and the pigment cells spread out to produce large color patches.

Blending In: Moths and Snails

An animal's color often matches its environment. This helps safeguard the animal against predators. The green Saturniid moth caterpillar and other caterpillars protect themselves by living among green leaves, where they're hard to detect. Dog whelks, a kind of snail (below), turn shades of yellow, pink, orange, and purple, depending on what they eat. This change helps them blend with their environments. Pale whelks eat light-colored barnacles, while darker whelks feed on dark-colored mussels.

Saturniid moth caterpillar

Dog whelks

Decapod crustaceans

Undetected: Shrimp

In deep ocean waters, bluish-black shrimp are not visible to fish and other predators. The ocean absorbs light rays—first red, then yellow, green, and blue—as they pass through it. Blue light penetrates the deepest, down to where bluish-black shrimp live. Shrimp appear red in the photo above because they reflect the red light of the photographer's camera lamp. Without the lamp, the shrimp are their normal dark, bluish-black color—and invisible to predators.

Stick Around: Walkingstick

Sometimes it's best to stick it out. The walkingstick, also called a stick insect, sticks it out by resembling a stick; it doesn't stick out to the predators that stick around in its habitat looking for a meal. Some species of walkingsticks also discourage predators with sharp spines, a bad odor, or eggs that look like seeds. A walkingstick can grow up to 12 inches (30 cm).

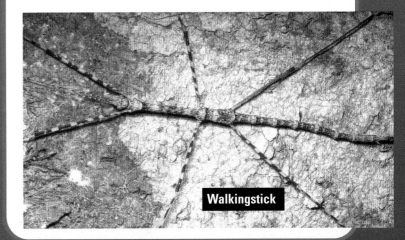

Walkingstick

Pesty Critters

Sometimes the smallest invertebrates can mean big trouble.

ZEBRA MUSSELS **Great Lakes, United States** Some invertebrates just won't let go. Take zebra mussels, mollusks that are quickly taking over the Great Lakes and spreading to rivers. Once found only in Eastern Europe, these mussels were released into the Great Lakes when visiting European ships flushed their ballast tanks. Zebra mussels live in colonies and attach themselves to hard surfaces. One mussel can produce up to a million offspring. These invertebrates clog pipes, destroy ship motors, and kill native clams by sticking to their shells.

NORTH AMERICA

SOUTH AMERICA

SEA URCHINS **Western Alaska, U.S.** Off the coast of Alaska, the number of sea otters, the sea urchin's natural predator, has declined, due, possibly, to pollution. That may be good news for sea urchins, but it's bad news for a balanced ecosystem. Sea urchins are overrunning the environment by eating all the seaweed. Fish and other creatures that depend on seaweed for food and habitat are leaving the area.

A dead sea urchin

JELLYFISH **Gulf of Mexico region** In June 2000, unusual ocean currents swept the Australian spotted jellyfish from the Caribbean Sea into the Gulf of Mexico. Plankton, a favorite jellyfish food, grows in huge quantities in the Gulf, and jellyfish have few predators there. The result is that massive jellyfish populations have taken over. One group covers an area the size of a football field. Jellyfish eat the young of all kinds of fish and shellfish, causing sharp declines in fish populations.

TICKS **Northeastern U.S.** Watch out for ticks the next time you take a hike. The tick, a kind of forest arachnid, feeds on human and animal blood. Ticks often attach themselves to humans and animals, including bears, deer, birds, and mice. Some ticks carry infectious bacteria, and they may transmit Lyme disease, which demands medical treatment. Ticks are tiny, so people often don't know they've been bitten until they experience a rash, a fever, or other symptoms of the disease. Lyme-disease-carrying ticks also live in western Europe.

ASIA

EUROPE

HOOKWORMS **Southern Asia** Careful where you walk! Hookworm larvae, which are found especially in human waste, can penetrate the skin of humans and animals and cause infection in the blood. Doctors are developing a vaccine, but, for now, improving waste disposal and medical services will help those in danger of getting the disease.

AFRICA

AUSTRALIA

THE MEDITERRANEAN FRUIT FLY (MEDFLY)

Mediterranean coast The medfly first started causing trouble in ancient times, in fields around the Mediterranean Sea. Today, it's also a problem in Africa, Europe, and Central and South America. Every year peaches, mangoes, oranges, and bananas are destroyed by the adult female medfly, which lays eggs inside fruit. When the eggs hatch, the larvae eat the fruit from the inside out.

Activity

WEB SIGHTS Pick a place you'd like to visit and research the invertebrates that live there. Choose one and find the following information about that animal: What does it eat? What are its predators? What is its habitat? How does the invertebrate affect the environment? Also, create a food web with your data. What would happen if this species were removed from the environment?

21

Go, Bug, Go!

Robert J. Full watches insects run across gelatin in his lab. Why? To create more efficient robots.

Biologist Robert J. Full

To design robots, Dr. Robert J. Full looks at nature for solutions to structural challenges. A biologist at the University of California, Berkeley, he examines the structures and motions of invertebrates to help him design high-tech robots that may save lives. "We're interested in discovering the secrets of nature," Full says. "We share what we've learned by teaching it to engineers, who use it for inspiration for new [robot] designs." The robot RHex, which is based on a cockroach's locomotion, might someday enter a burning building to find people trapped inside. Ariel, a robot based on a crab's movements, may find dangerous unexploded land and water mines.

To explain how the structural design of invertebrates is valuable to robotics, the science of making robots, Full says, "If you have a lot of legs on the ground, it's harder to tip over. If those legs are also springy, then when you hit bumps, you very quickly bounce back to where you were. And you don't need a big fancy brain to do it." He applies this information to robots.

Centipede on a Treadmill

To understand how an animal's structure helps it move, Full measures the forces that produce motion and the motion itself.

He observes a centipede running on a tiny treadmill and photographs it with five high-speed cameras. Full feeds the information from the photos into a computer that shows the animal's movement. "It's the same technique you use to make people move around in a video game," says Full, "except, instead of just playing, we're studying the velocity and angle of the [insect's] motion."

Full observes a centipede running on a treadmill.

Full observes a cockroach running across gelatin so he can measure the force of the insect's legs. He puts filters, which are like sunglasses, on both sides of the gelatin and shines a light through it. As the roach steps and puts pressure on the gelatin, the amount of light shining through increases. The pressure of the insect's feet changes as it runs, and Full measures the changing amounts of light.

A cockroach moves forward using three of its six legs at a time—front and back legs on one side and the middle leg on the other. With three legs touching the ground at one time, the animal remains balanced and stable. Its locomotion method is also efficient. For its size, the cockroach is the fastest species on Earth. Its speed is equivalent to a person running 220 miles (354 km) an hour!

From Roaches to Robots

Full applies to robots what he learns about cockroaches, such as their ease in moving over bumpy surfaces. RHex "can go over sand, brush, grass, and stones," says Full. "No wheeled vehicle could do that." Full's research may even go into designing the next robots for space exploration.

Full's work with invertebrates inspires scientists and engineers to imagine a future with helpful and useful robots.

A graduate student in Full's lab maneuvers the robot RHex using remote control.

Bugs R Us

To people, moving is more than just getting around. How we move can convey how we think and feel. To create the insect characters in the movie *A Bug's Life*, the moviemakers consulted Dr. Full for his expert opinion. They weren't just trying to figure out how insects move. They wanted to use insect movement to express emotion and personality in their characters. For example, the animators used the springlike motion of the tobacco hornworm to express happiness in Heimlich, the caterpillar.

Activity

ANIMAL ANDROIDS Robert J. Full worked with middle school students to create robots. Check out their Web site: polypedal.berkeley.edu/Oak_Grove/OG_home.html. Form teams of 3 or 4 students and choose an invertebrate that interests you. What kind of robot would you build based on the animal's movements?

SPARE *Parts*

Life is not possible without growth. Look at your skin. New cells produced at an inner level eventually reach the surface, where they are shed. That's when new skin grows in its place. This is why your tan fades and the scrape on your knee heals. The process is called regeneration, which is the replacement of old tissue with new tissue.

Invertebrates regenerate to an amazing degree. Scientists think that specialized cells develop in these animals, possibly stimulated by the nervous system, wherever a part is lost. These cells multiply and make up the tissues that become the regenerated part.

Find out why regeneration is so important to invertebrates' survival in a world filled with predators.

LETTING GO

If a predator bites an octopus's arm, the octopus can escape by leaving its wriggling arm in the predator's mouth. The wound does not bleed because vessels quickly contract to stop the flow of blood. In about six weeks, the octopus grows a new arm. On the down side, before it regrows its arm, the octopus is more vulnerable to attack. Also, it must use more energy than usual to help the new arm grow.

FULLY ARMED

The sea star, usually called a starfish, is an echinoderm (ee-KINE-uh-derm), a spiny-skinned animal with thick arms radiating from a round body or central disk. All species live in the ocean, and most have five arms. A sea star can drop an arm if it must escape to defend itself, and a shorter arm will grow in its place. Badly injured sea stars can regenerate other parts of their bodies, too. As long as one-fifth of the sea star's body remains, a new animal grows. If the animal is torn into five parts, five new sea stars will develop.

Plan A Head

Planarian (pluh-NARE-ee-an) flatworms live in water, damp soil, and under rocks and other objects.

The planarian moves slowly and has a soft body, so it isn't well protected against predators. Even so, it's built to survive and can regenerate any lost or damaged body part. If a bird pulls it in two, the planarian will grow a new "head" section or a new "back" section. Many worm species can regenerate by dividing into two pieces; each develops into a complete new adult.

Planarian flatworms range in length from 1/4 inch (0.6 cm) to 1 1/2 inches (3.75 cm) long.

Activity

HEADS OR TAILS? Go to the library or search the Internet to research other animals that can regenerate. Examples are sponges, hydras, segmented worms, lobsters, crayfish, and insects. Create a table showing the data you've collected. How do these animals regenerate? Are there similarities and differences across species? What are the advantages and disadvantages of this adaptation?

DIRT DIGGER

You're an earthworm wriggling around under a vegetable garden. You're small, but you have special ways of getting around. Let's see you do your stuff.

You're about 18 inches (46 cm) underground, in soil that is warm and moist. *Ah, just right!* You move easily through the soil, aided by the slime covering your body. It's called mucus, and it also helps you breathe. Like most invertebrates, you don't have lungs. You breathe through the entire surface of your body, and the mucus lets you absorb air. Without it, you'd dry up and die. The warm soil also keeps you moist and able to move and breathe. If the dirt were too dry or cold, you would burrow deeper until it felt right.

You're an average earthworm. Your body is divided into more than 100 segments, each able to move independently. You move by, first, stretching out long and thin, using the short muscles that circle your body in each segment. Then you use your long muscles, the ones that run lengthwise through your body, to pull yourself together. *Strrreeetch. Pull together. Strrreeetch.* Bits of dirt fall over you as you push through your tunnel and curve around rocks, rotting twigs, and plant roots.

Suddenly the ground is slippery. Aboveground, it's soaking wet, and you're beginning to feel it. Someone must have turned on the sprinkler! To get through the mud, out come your tiny bristles, called setae (set-AY), that grip the soil and propel you in any direction. You push them out or pull them in as needed.

Worm Expressway

Excuse me! Pardon me! Can I get by, please? Suddenly it's a superhighway down here, with lots of earthworms going in every direction. This large vegetable plot, covering about an acre, contains anywhere from 50,000 to a million worms. Making sharp turns is easy for you, since you have no bones or hard outer covering. You're lucky

An earthworm "sees" the light at the end of the tunnel.

you can turn so fast, because you're always dodging the gardener's tools and underground animals, such as shrews and moles, that would love a tasty earthworm for dinner.

Mmmm! All around you are rotten leaves mixed in with moist soil. You keep wriggling and eating the soil, until you locate something delicious. Open wide! Your long upper lip pulls in a yummy decayed leaf. The leaf moves into your gizzard and then into your intestine, which takes up most of your body. Your intestine absorbs the nutrients you need, and then you push the remaining waste, called castings, out your back end.

You've just dropped some castings, which are rich in nutrients, near a group of tomato plant roots. Your castings help the plants grow, and your burrowing has loosened the dirt so they can spread their roots.

Danger Ahead

You're still hungry, so you head for the surface. As your front end breaks through, light strikes you, sending you burrowing back into the dirt. You couldn't "see" the light, but you sensed it through your "eyespots," which are special cells located on your outer skin. You try again later. No more light. It's safe to surface. After anchoring your tail end in your tunnel, you grope around for food. *Whoosh!* You duck back inside your tunnel just in time. That was close—you were almost a bird's snack! You have no ears, so you couldn't hear it, but your skin felt the vibrations of the bird's hopping feet.

Once it's safe again, you stick your front end out of your tunnel, poking around again for food. You stretch out. Still keeping your tail in your tunnel, you stretch until your mouth brushes across a decaying flower. Wiggling backwards, you pull a petal back down into your burrow to eat in safety. As you munch, a sense of deep satisfaction comes over you. *Ah, dessert!*

Activity

A WORM'S VIEW Cut the top off a plastic 2-liter bottle and place a small, glass jar at the bottom of the bottle. Pour moist soil in the bottle and wrap black construction paper around the bottle. Add leaves, bits of apple core, or potato peels. Add earthworms. You can find worms in garden soil, or you can purchase worms by mail. The small jar creates a "wall" that will force the worms close to the side of the bottle, through which you can watch them. Poke holes in a paper plate and place it over the top of the bottle. In low light, remove the construction paper to observe your worms. Replace the paper when you're finished. How do the worms feed? How do they react to brighter light?

Treasure-Hunt Horrors

"You must be crazy if you think I'm going in there!" said Pearl Shelley defiantly, as she kicked the soccer ball up in the air and caught it. "I don't care if there is some old pirate's treasure in the abandoned woodshed by old Widow Fiddleboch's house." Casting a doubtful glance at the dilapidated shack, she said, "The place gives me the creeps. I don't want to go anywhere near it."

"Mrs. Fiddleboch's been so reclusive, I don't think she's used that shed for years," said Perry Winkler as they walked by. "What harm could it do to look for a little pirate treasure?"

"Yeah, have a little backbone, Pearl," nudged her friend Luke Vermes. "It's just that old Mr.

Fiddleboch was a merchant sailor and loved to tell pirate stories. Rumor has it that he found some treasures and stowed them away in the woodshed."

"Rumor has it," corrected Pearl, "that whatever treasure he found had a curse on it, and anyone who encounters it has bad luck. Just look at the woods behind her house. You know they're probably infested with deer ticks. Those little blood suckers are really small and hard to see—most people don't even know when they get bitten. That happened to my cousin. She just woke up one day with a bulls-eye rash, a fever, and achy joints. No thanks! I'll bet the woodshed is filled with other scary creatures, too."

"Oh, don't be such a scaredy-cat," said Perry. "Ticks don't scare me, and neither do tall tales or curses. If it's just a matter of peeking in the woodshed for some pirate treasure, I'll do it," he announced. Perry left his friends on the sidewalk and darted toward the woodshed. Less than three minutes later, he bounded back with a mysterious grin on his face.

"Did you see anything?" chimed Pearl and Luke in unison.

"Yeah, I think I found the treasure you've heard about. But I've gotta run. I promised to help out with weekend chores this morning. I'll tell you about it at

soccer practice tonight!" Perry ran down the road before his friends could say another word.

Several hours later, after the evening's practice, Luke met up with Pearl. "No sign of Perry, huh?" he asked.

"Actually," Pearl frowned, "I couldn't wait to hear what Perry found in the woodshed, so I called him just before practice. He sounded awful! I barely had a chance to talk to him before his mom picked up the phone and explained that he'd suddenly come down with fever, chills, and vomiting. She was just getting ready to take him to the hospital."

"Oh, no!" Luke gasped. "He looked perfectly fine when we saw him. Do you think it has something to do with what he found?"

"I don't know," said Pearl. "Perry told me the pirate booty he found was nothing more than an old copy of *Treasure Island*. The only other thing he mentioned was that the skin on his fingertip had just started stinging and swelling."

"Hmm," Luke paused. "This doesn't sound good. We should investigate."

"Y-you mean go into the woodshed?" stammered Pearl.

"Don't worry, we'll stick together," Luke assured her. "Let's just see if we can find anything suspicious that might help explain what happened to Perry."

Less than an hour later, flashlights in hand, the two friends were retracing Perry's steps in the old woodshed.

"Yikes! See, I told you this place is full of creepy crawlers," shrieked Pearl, pointing to a long-legged harvestman creeping along the dusty floor.

"Oh, that's just a kind of daddy longlegs. It's not really a true spider at all. It doesn't even produce silk to make webs," Luke said. "Hey, did you hear that cricket? I'll bet those stacks of wood are home to more than one of those critters."

"Look over here in the corner," Pearl said, shining her light on several wooden crates. "You can tell Perry unstacked these and wiped away the dust and cobwebs. I'll bet this is where he found that book."

Luke brushed away a few broken strands of an irregular spider web with off-white, silky sacs as he reached for the dusty book and thumbed through it. "Nothing suspicious here," he muttered. As he put the book back, he snagged his shirtsleeve on the tip of a rusty tack poking out of the crate. "Ouch!"

"Careful," warned Pearl. "Even if there's no real treasure, I don't want us to get any bad luck." As she shined the light on Luke's sleeve, she saw a small brown arachnid crawl into the shadows of the box. "Cool! It looked like it had a little violin painted on its back."

"Let's get out of here," said Luke. "This place is starting to give me the creeps, too." He shined the light around the woodshed one last time to make sure they didn't miss anything.

Pearl watched her friend brush dust and a few sticky silk threads off his shirtsleeve. "Luke!" she said with sudden conviction, "I think I know what happened to Perry. I just want to look something up in my *Big Book of Bugs* at home. Let's go to my place!"

After Pearl and Luke did more research and found pictures of some of the suspect critters in the woodshed, they had a pretty good idea about what happened to Perry and called his mom right away. Check out the clues below to see if you can solve the mystery of Perry's sudden illness.

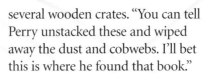

Daddy Longlegs
Class: Arachnida. **Order:** Opiliones. Eats small insects, snails, worms, fruit and vegetable matter. Stinky fluid secretions may cause slight allergic reactions in some people.

Brown Recluse
Class: Arachnida. **Order:** Araneae. Builds irregular webs. Feeds on small insects and cockroaches. Venomous bite can cause swelling and tissue death.

Tick
Class: Arachnida. **Order:** Acari. Parasite. Feeds on blood of birds, mice, deer, dogs, humans, and other mammals.

Answer on page 32

SPINELESS LIVES

MEETING AND GREETING

Invertebrates have many ways of meeting and greeting.

⌃ Some butterflies can tell who's who by their markings. For example, some males have two dots on their wings, while some females have one.

⌃ Although most flatworm species are both male and female, a flatworm can't fertilize itself. When two flatworms mate, they exchange sperm so the eggs of both worms are fertilized.

⌃ Many sponges have the ability to reproduce as either a female or a male, increasing their chances of creating a new sponge. Throughout its life, a sponge can play both the female and male roles. The male sponge releases sperm, which enters the female. After the sponge is fertilized, the larvae are released and drift for a few days. They then land on a surface and start to grow.

Orange sponge—male or female?

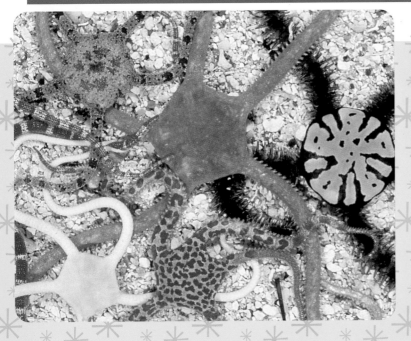

BYE-BYE BABIES

Like many marine animals, brittle stars (left) never get to see their mothers. In spring and summer, brittle stars release millions of eggs, which develop into larvae. The larvae float in the water for three weeks, then settle to the bottom of a shallow tide pool. The animal's name comes from its brittle arms, which can break off easily. New arms, however, grow in their place.

Playing Defense

Not having a backbone, invertebrates have found other ways to get by. To protect themselves in their environments, they have evolved special features. Most know how to deal with threats from other creatures. Here are some tough invertebrates.

- Scuttlers are crabs that act like they know how to fight back. Sometimes gulls or other predators try to eat a scuttler's legs. The crab strikes a series of poses meant to scare away its predator. First, it shows caution. Then it crouches and pretends to attack. Finally, it retreats. Boxer crabs carry around stinging anemones in their pincers to defend themselves. They wave their pincers at any threatening creature.

- Squids use color to communicate. Dark colors signal aggression, glittering silver means hostility, and pale patterns usually indicate that the squid is escaping a predator.

- Limpets are champions. These creatures live on rocky shores pounded by waves. To survive, they have developed hard outer shells and a good grip. Using the side of its shell, a limpet digs a pit in the rock. It uses a "foot" on the underside of its body to stick to the stone.

Atlantic oval squid

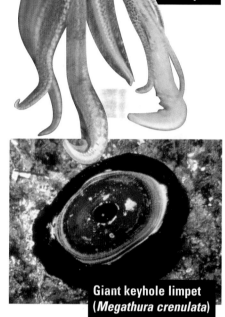

Giant keyhole limpet
(*Megathura crenulata*)

Jokes With No Backbone

What do you call a mosquito with a tin suit? — A bite in shining armor.

What did one octopus say to the other octopus? — I want to hold your hand, hand, hand, hand, hand, hand, hand, hand.

Did you hear about the two silkworms that had a race? — It ended in a tie.

What's in the middle of a jellyfish? — A jellybutton.

Why didn't the lobster share its toys? — It was too shellfish.

Why do bees have sticky hair? — Because they have honeycombs.

What did the bug say when it hit the windshield? — I don't have the guts to do that again.

YOUR WORLD YOUR TURN

Invertebrates Unite

Invertebrates are diverse creatures that make up a large part of the animal kingdom and live in every ecosystem of the world. Like all animals, invertebrates have evolved special features that enable them to survive in their environments.

Choose five invertebrates from the same ecosystem, such as the land surrounding your school, or a seashore, fresh-water, pond, or marsh environment. Form teams. Each team should study one invertebrate from this ecosystem. Consider the following questions.

- What is this animal's most interesting feature?
- What special structures enable it to survive?
- How does it protect itself?
- What is its habitat?
- Is this the only type of environment it lives in? If not, where else could you find it?
- How has it adapted to this environment?
- How does it reproduce?
- What are its predators? What is its prey?
- Does it affect people? If so, how?
- How do people affect this animal?
- Is this animal native to its environment or has it migrated to this area?

Use the data you've collected to make a large chart of invertebrates. Try to match them up. Can you make any connections between these animals? Some might compete for the same food, some are predators, and some are prey. A few influence the environment; others do not. Some invertebrates don't connect with any other invertebrates at all.

After you've had a class discussion, ask other schools to participate. Swap your chart with their chart. Compare the similarities and contrast the differences. What have you learned from other students? Would you have approached your animal in the same way? A different way? Why or why not?

ANSWER Solve-It-Yourself Mystery, pages 28–29

Perry was suffering from the bite of a venomous spider. The culprit was a brown recluse spider, commonly known as the violin spider or fiddleback because of the violin-shaped pattern on its head region. The brown recluse is a shy invertebrate that likes to hide in undisturbed areas, such as basements, attics, and woodpiles. Pearl saw Luke brush away the spider web with silky egg sacs. Perry was probably bitten when he picked up the copy of *Treasure Island*, which was stored in the crate where the spider had made its home. The spider's venom contains a poison that can result in blood and tissue damage. Like many people who suffer from spider bites, Perry didn't notice the bite right away, but several hours later complained of a stinging sensation and swelling on his finger, where he was bitten. The fever, chills, and nausea were also symptoms of the spider bite.

In addition to providing a secluded shelter to make a home, the woodshed turned out to be a good place for the brown recluse to find food, such as the crickets Luke and Pearl heard.